All the photos in this book were taken on location at Burning Man
For many years we returned annually to take portraits at the Burning Man event. Our studio consisted of this tent and a nine-foot white paper backdrop.

Tell your friends
This book was published thanks to the contributions of hundreds of people who value creativity, open-mindedness, culture jamming, and joy. If you also appreciate this photo project and want it to bring forth change, you can help by showing it around. To see the video fun, and to introduce your online friends to the project, go here to take a peek at:

www.ThePeopleOfBurningMan.com

welcome

Burning Man: For one week a year, tens of thousands of people create a temporary city in the desert. Commerce is banned. Creativity, absurdity, spirituality, and an extreme sense of freedom prevail.

do you allow yourself to be free?

Is self expression

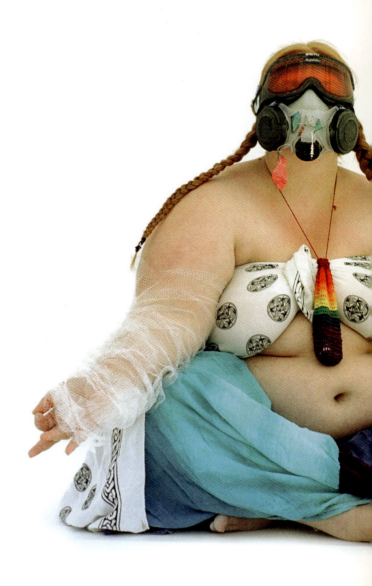

vital

who do you love?

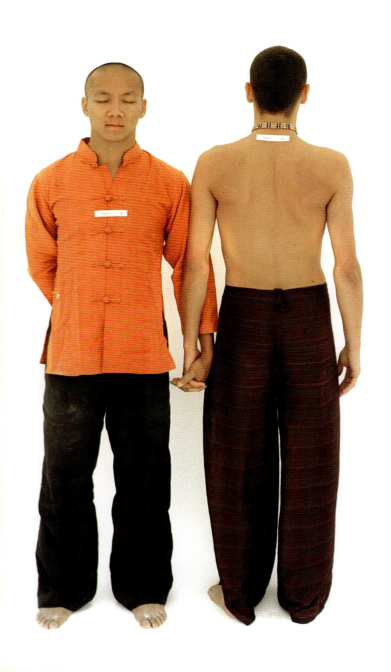

this book

loves

YOU

Love

It is so yummy to love and to be loved. How much love do you have to give?

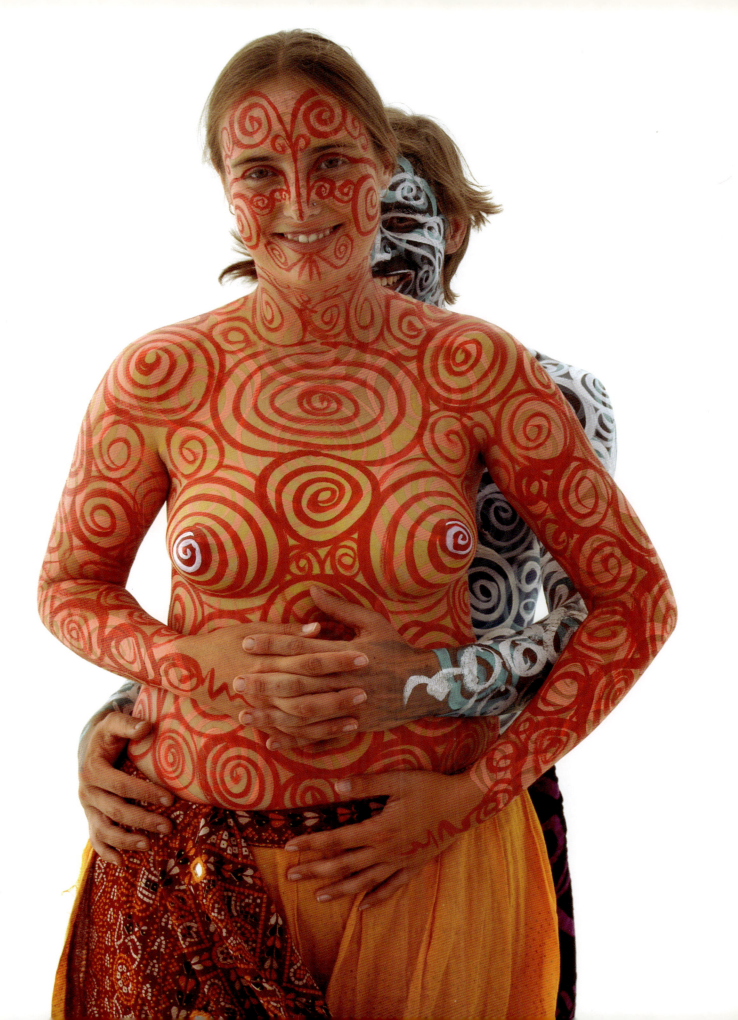

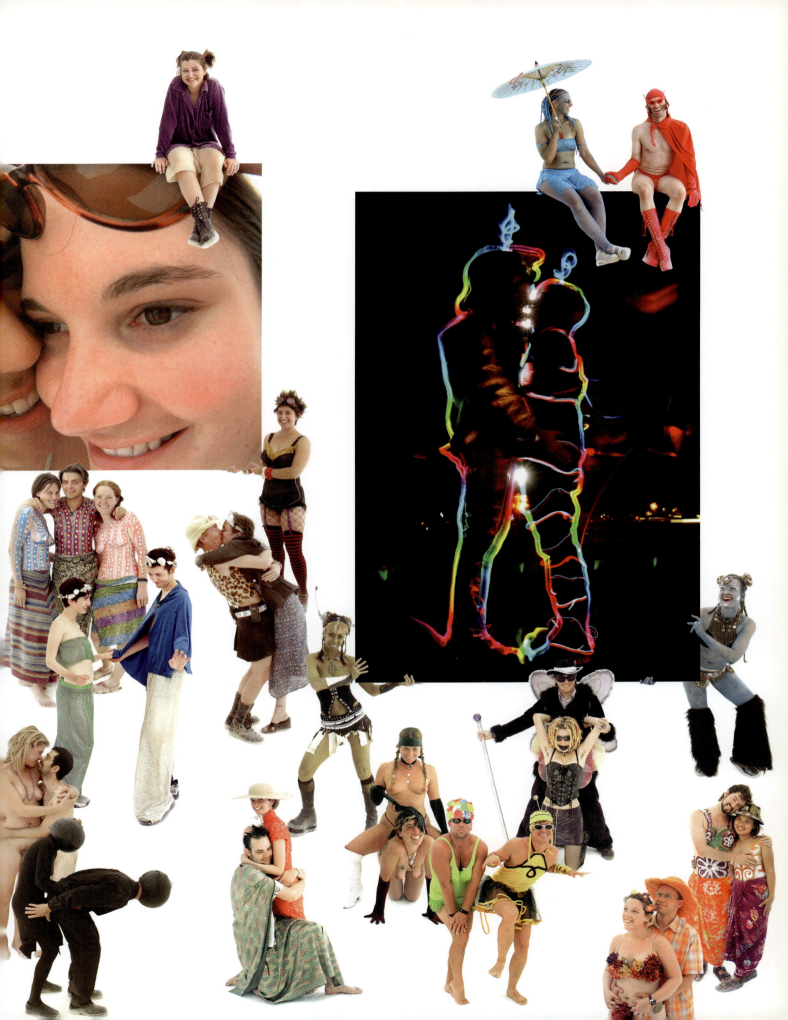

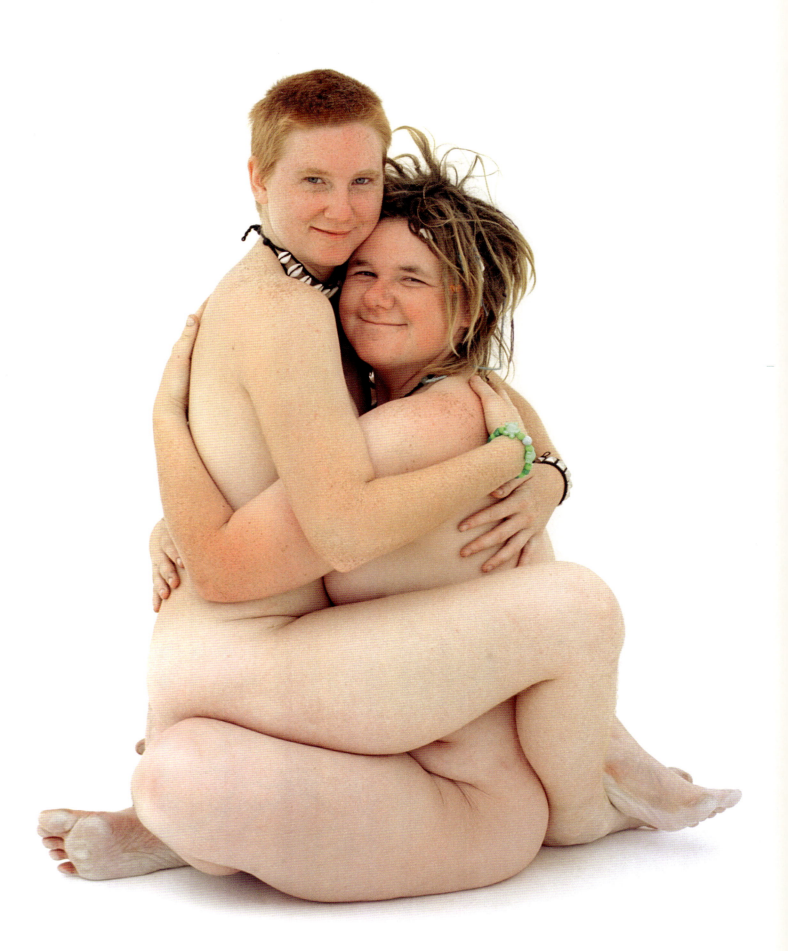

self expression

Your joy will save you.
Your love.
Your rage.
Your creativity.
Your self.

Match the faces with the tattoos

Hints: "16" is a portrait of the person. "F" has a back tattoo. "9" is wearing a hat. "2" is wearing earrings. Sandwichgirl has two pairs of glasses. "D" has many tattoos that are inspired by the movie "Fight Club".

More hints: "M" has been HIV+ for 20 years. "K" runs a store called "bunnywarez". "C" is in the "Creators" chapter. The answers are listed upside down on the line below this.

Answers: A-3, B-7, C-12, D-1, E-14, F-11, G-13, H-6, I-5, J-2, K-15, L-16, M-4, N-9, O-8, F-10.

vaLues

What business are you in?

Match the job with the person.

1. Computer Programmer
2. Theatre Student
3. Attorney
4. Another Attorney
5. Real Estate Agent
6. Movie Actor
7. Tax Accountant
8. Photography Agent
9. Import Boutique Owner

Hints: "RTFM" stands for "Read The Fucking Manual." The Photo Agent shows up very early in the book. The two Attorneys are next to each other. One of the Attorneys is in the "Body" chapter. The Real Estate Agent is on the "Groups" page in the "Burning Man" chapter. The Actor and colorful Boutique Owner are wearing glasses. The Theatre Student is topless. The answers are at the bottom of the page.

Answers: A-8, B-7, C-2, D-5, E-9, F-3 or 4, G-3 or 4, H-1, I-6 (She's in Troma films.)

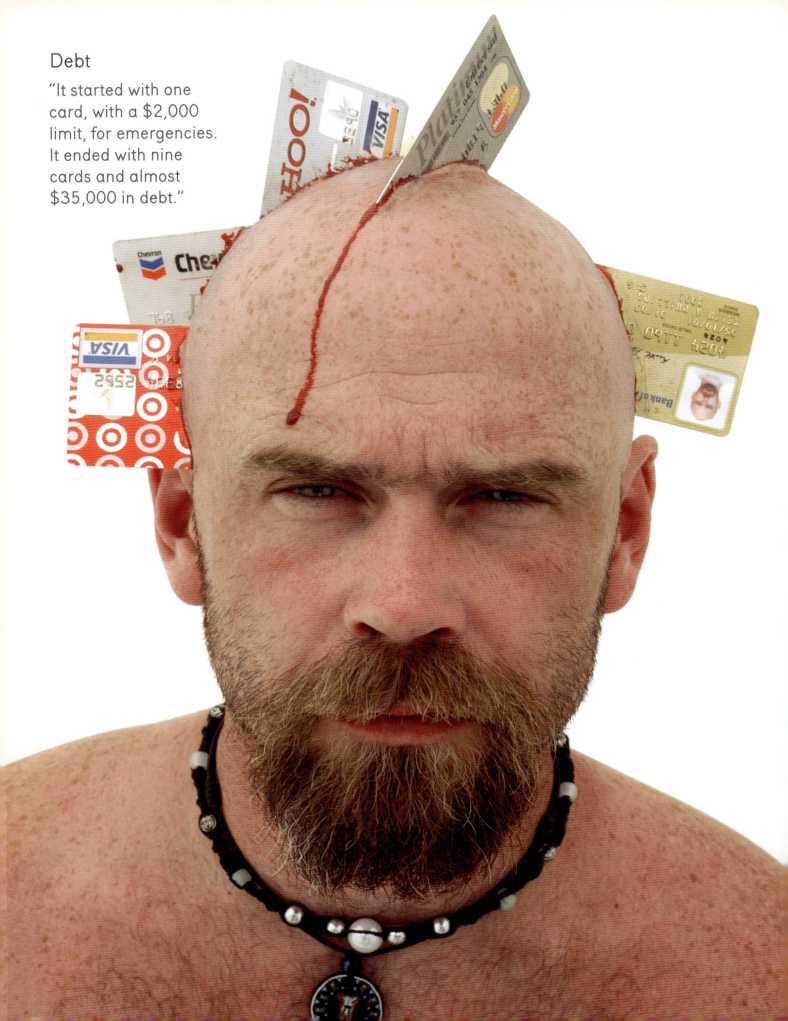

Debt

"It started with one card, with a $2,000 limit, for emergencies. It ended with nine cards and almost $35,000 in debt."

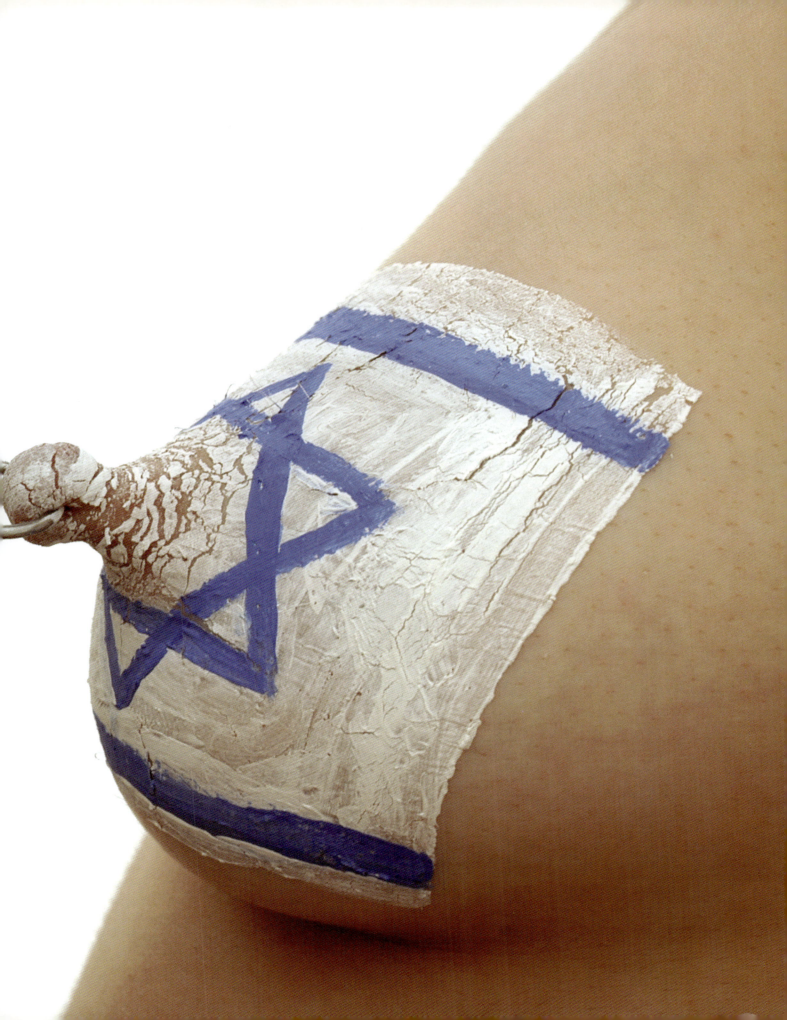

Student disciplined for refusing the pledge

Stephan Clark
Record-Bee staff

On Oct. 28, Kearney says her son was told by his teacher that he should "find another school to go to if he doesn't want to stand for the pledge," and that he would receive detention if he continued to refuse, according to a Nov. 7 complaint Kearney filed with the school district.

The following day, after again refusing to stand, Woodbury was sent to the school's administrative office, according to the complaint.

The next week, Woodbury confronted his teacher with a packet of information supporting his Constitutional right not to participate in the pledge, Kearney said.

But his teacher, according to Kearney's complaint, responded by throwing the information into a trash can and saying, "I don't care what the law is. Get out of my class if you're not going to say the Pledge!"

With a daughter one grade behind her son, Kearney said she is continuing to forward her complaint to ensure that children in the future will not be made to feel unpatriotic while exercising their Constitutional right not to recite the pledge.

"He's the patriot in this thing," she said of her son. "He's pushing the envelope, standing up for the unpopular position."

The state education code requires that patriotic exercises be conducted daily at public elementary and secondary schools; however, federal courts, in such cases as West Virginia State Board of Education et al v. Barnette et al, have held that individuals may not be compelled to salute the flag or to stand during the salute.

Woodbury said his reasons for not wanting to salute the flag are political.

"The reason I don't want to stand for the pledge is that I believe the flag has become a symbol of the government, and I believe the government right now is corrupt," he said.

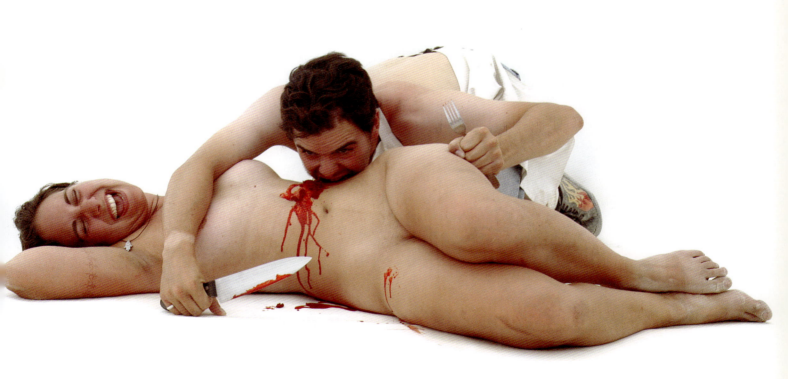

"Calamity Jane" a.k.a. Jerri Manthey
Actress and Burner expresses her sometimes difficult relationship with television.

burning man

A few glimpses for you of the event called Burning Man, and some of the characters who help give it life.

Larry Harvey
In 1986 he helped found Burning Man on a San Francisco beach, and has guided its progress ever since.

Danger Ranger, Ambassador

Founded the Black Rock Rangers in 1992. Part of the San Francisco Cacophony Society, which adopted and catapulted Burning Man early in the event's history. Ex-combat veteran and federal fugitive.

$teven Ra$pa as FLARE

"3,000 years and the playa is still dusty as hell." Flare vacuumed the desert, extension cord trailing behind. $teven organizes and supports year-round Burning Man community events.

Harley K. Dubois

Harley does a lot. She places all services, camps, and villages; manages ingress and egress; manages the volunteers; and oversees Playa Information, Greeters, Recycling, Earth Guardians, the Lamplighters, the Bus Depot, Town Meetings, and many staff meetings and functions. As Director of the Playa Safety Team, Harley oversees the Rangers, the Gate and Perimeter, and the Emergency Services Department.

Amanda, Skydiver

"I'm alive when I'm skydiving. Everything is clear. I'm at my best. To me it just seems natural. We soar through the air in our dreams. Why not live those dreams?"

Your Outfit

Every day is a fashion show.

Lamplighters

Each evening at Burning Man, as darkness approaches, a solemn group of white-robed individuals with poles slung over their shoulders wind their way through the city. They hang lit lanterns, full of fuel, on the lamp posts to provide illumination for the city.

Ministry of Statistics
This Theme Camp gathered the information on this page.

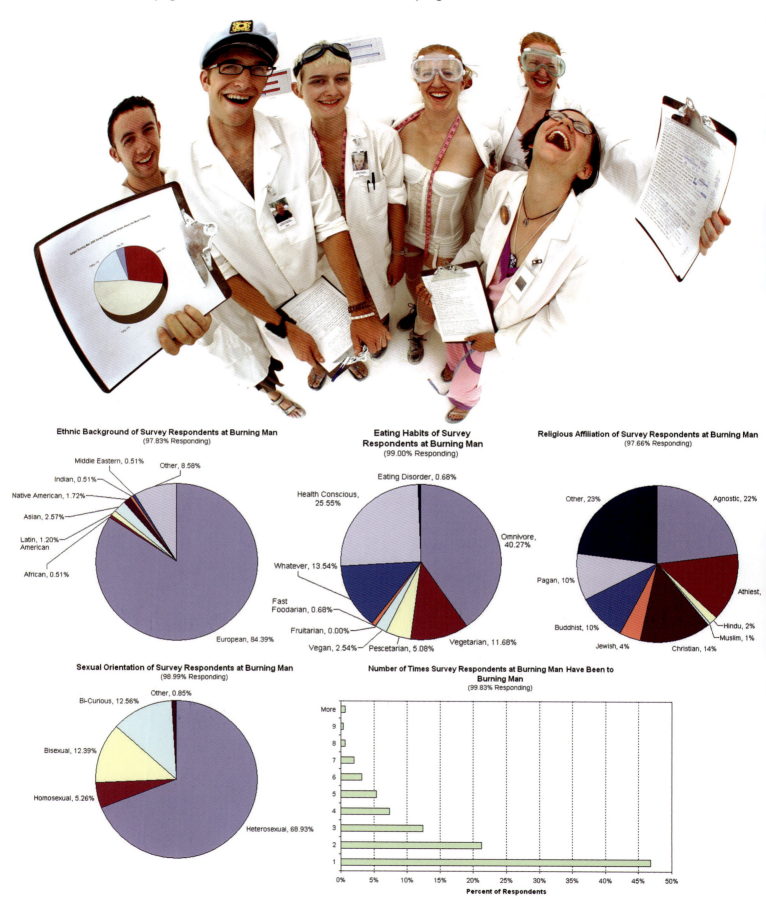

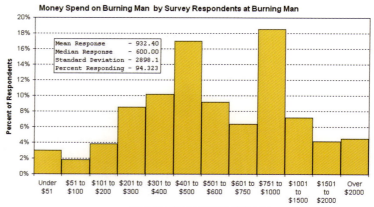
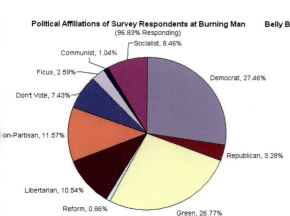
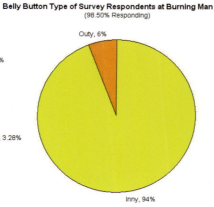
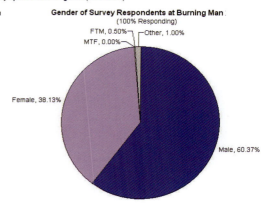
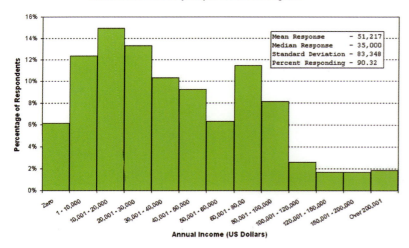
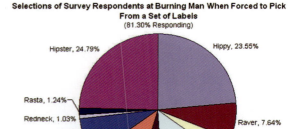
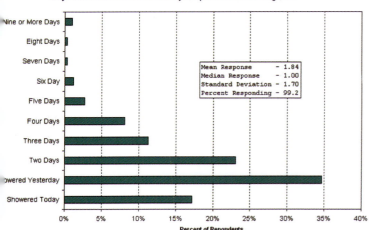
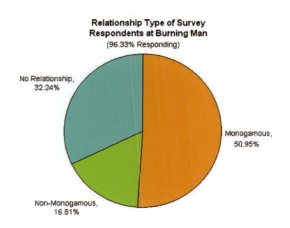

It's about respect

Photographers owe it to the world to help promote good, non-selfish camera etiquette. Nudity is not an invitation. Never take photographs of semi-clad people without asking first. Respect an answer of "no."

Wearing her community

Many people form Theme Camps. Some form Villages. People in the Gigsville Village make trading cards about themselves. Linda Parker made this dress out of a set of Gigsville cards.

Tourists

At Burning Man, everybody is highly encouraged to participate. People who don't are sometimes called "tourists."

fire

Burning is both death and rebirth.

The Temple

A loved one has died. You write on the Temple wall about how you miss them. You put a photograph of them and something of theirs into the temple. Sunday night, the Temple burns.

David Best
He built the first Temple, with a team of volunteers, the same year that his father died.

The story of the "Little Man"

In 1970, I found a little bamboo and metal amulet with a Chinese inscription reading "Mark of goodwill." I wore it next to my heart daily. In 1978, my son Bob was born. He and I were two peas in a pod. In 2000, at the age of 22, he died suddenly. As I viewed his body in the final moments before his remains were cremated, I suddenly was struck by a deep and primal wish to remove my little man from next to my heart and place it next to my son's still heart. I was struck with a sense of knowing that 30 years ago I had begun preparing for the death of my child eight years before he was ever conceived. I felt that I had known and even agreed to this profound experience on some level.

With the expressed blessing of the man who was to cremate my son, I placed my little man with my son's body to be turned to ash and molten metal.

In the months that followed, I grieved not only for my son, but also for the empty spot next to my heart.

Although I was happy to have a part of me go with my son, I missed my man of goodwill.

Six months later I took Bob's ashes to San Francisco. He had once told me that in the event of his death, he wanted his remains to be divided among his friends and then scattered along the 17-Mile Drive in Carmel. It was agonizing sifting through his ashes as I portioned them into vials. My heart stopped as I hit something solid. I thought it was the roof of his mouth, and I was almost horrified. It was my bamboo and metal amulet, unscathed, only much darker, and with a different patina. My little man had taken my son on his journey and had come back home to me!

John Willys "Bob" McGaha
1978 – 2000

Dr. MegaVolt

Dr. Austin Richards, physicist, is best known for riding around on top of a customized truck, seemingly using a giant Tesla coil to electrocute himself. People follow him like he's the Pied Piper, chanting, "We love you, Dr. MegaVolt!"

His specially made suit is a Faraday cage that channels the electricity harmlessly around his body. If any part of him protrudes from the suit during a performance, he dies.

danger

Danger, life, death, fear, bravery, pain, and awareness are all tied together. The same fear that helps to keep you alive also limits how fully you live and appreciate life.

Dust storm　　　　　　　　　　Visibility 15'

Backflip

A split second before he broke his nose.

The Med Tent

Two dehydration victims kneel before their doctor, who has saved them both from heat stroke. Their hands are bandaged from having had IV tubes in them. The Medical Tent is a small field clinic. His necklaces are gifts from grateful patients.

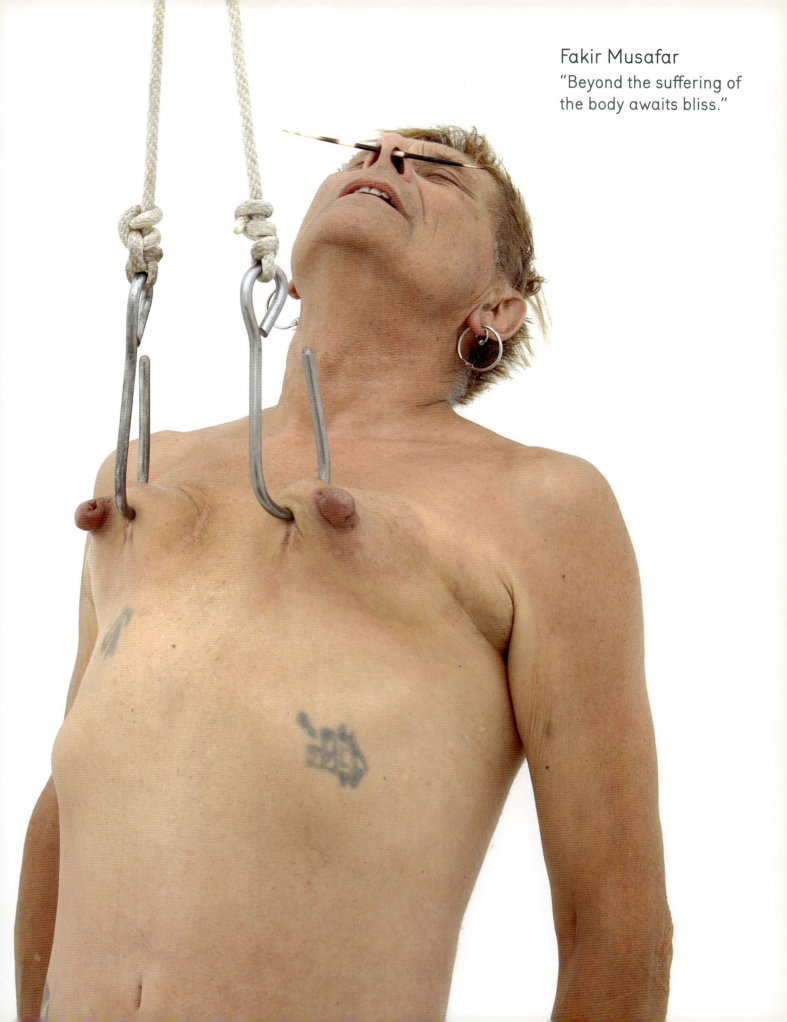

Fakir Musafar
"Beyond the suffering of the body awaits bliss."

the body

From early on, society teaches you to hide your body. Breaking free of one mental bond can help you break free of others.

Be good to yourself.
Be brave. Be safe.

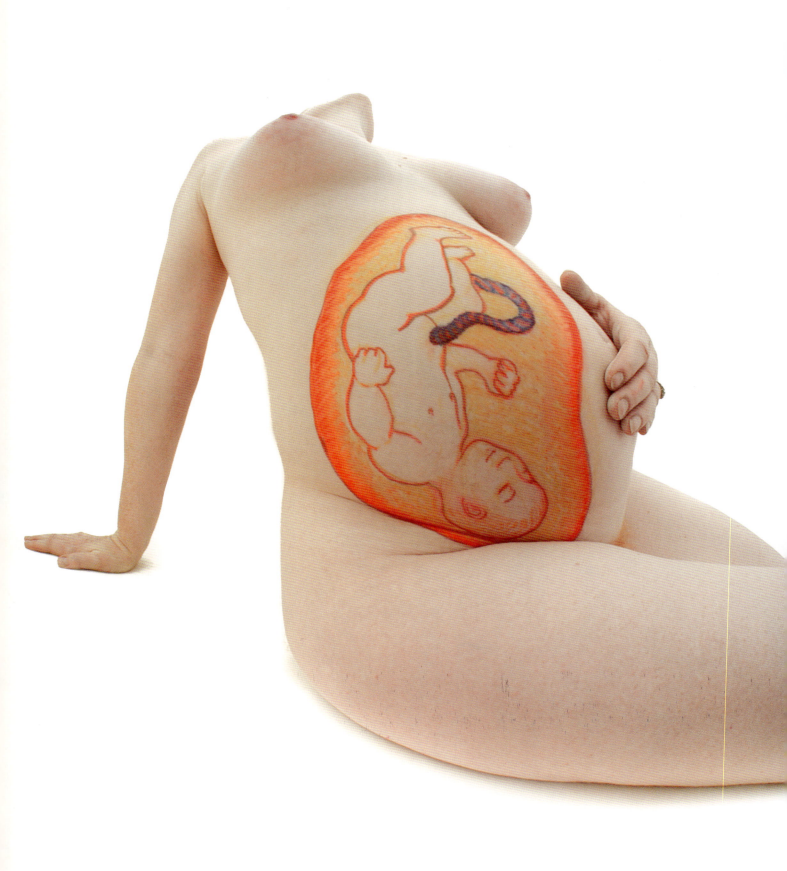

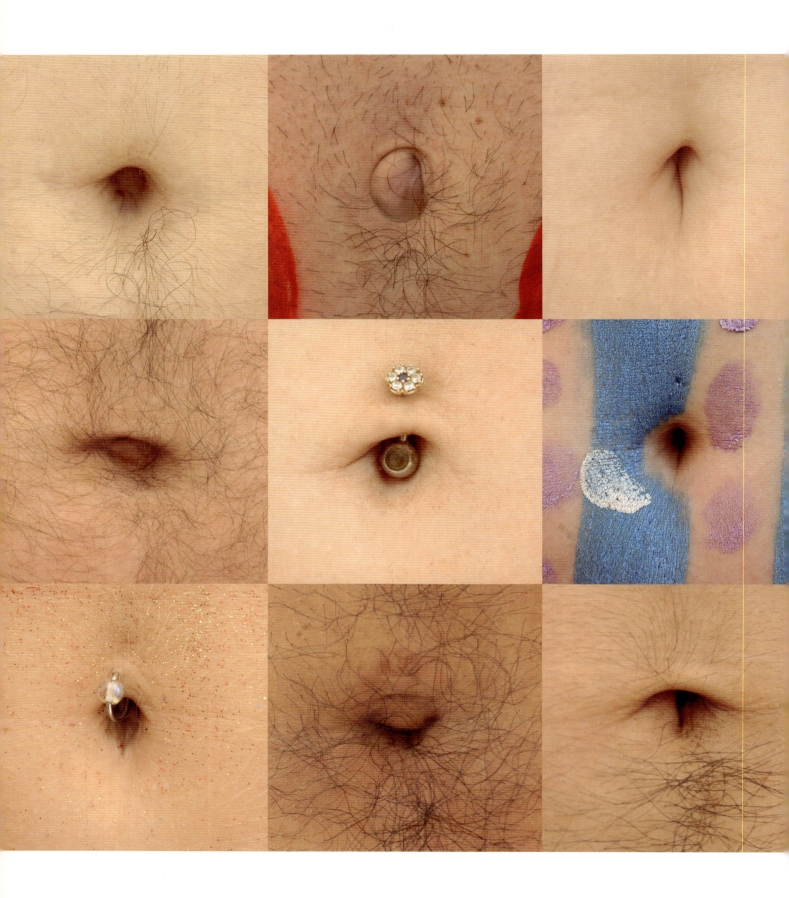

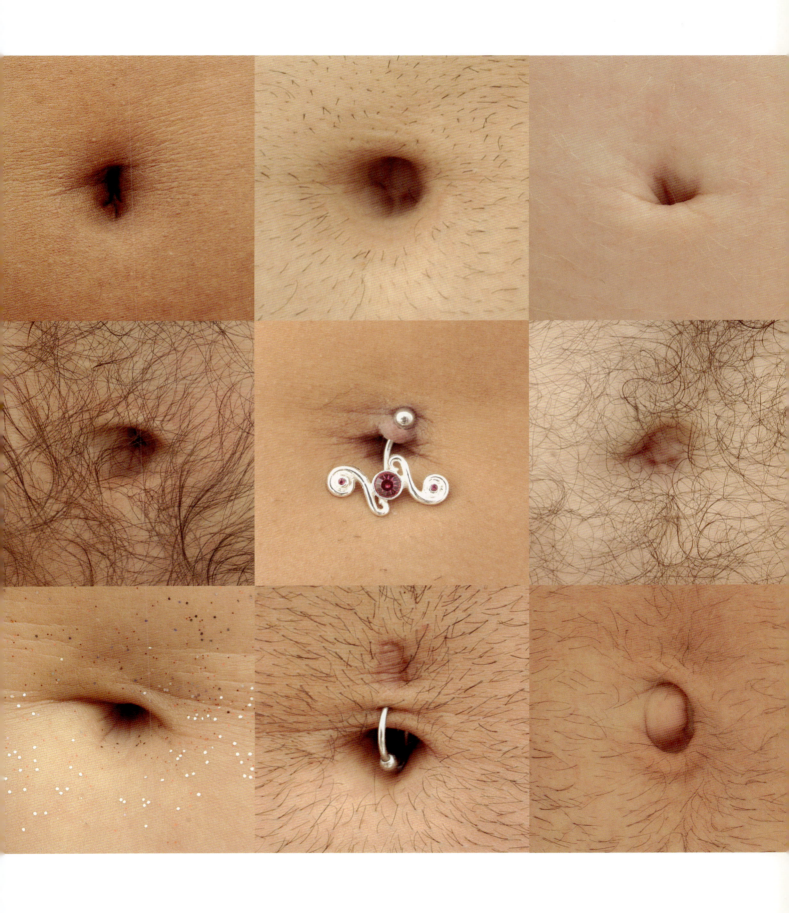

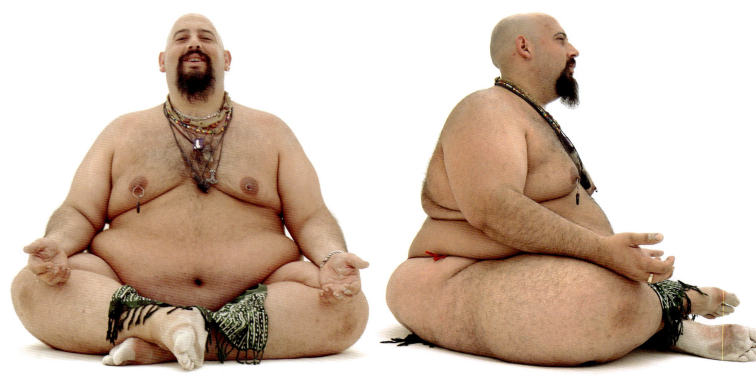

Playa Buddha

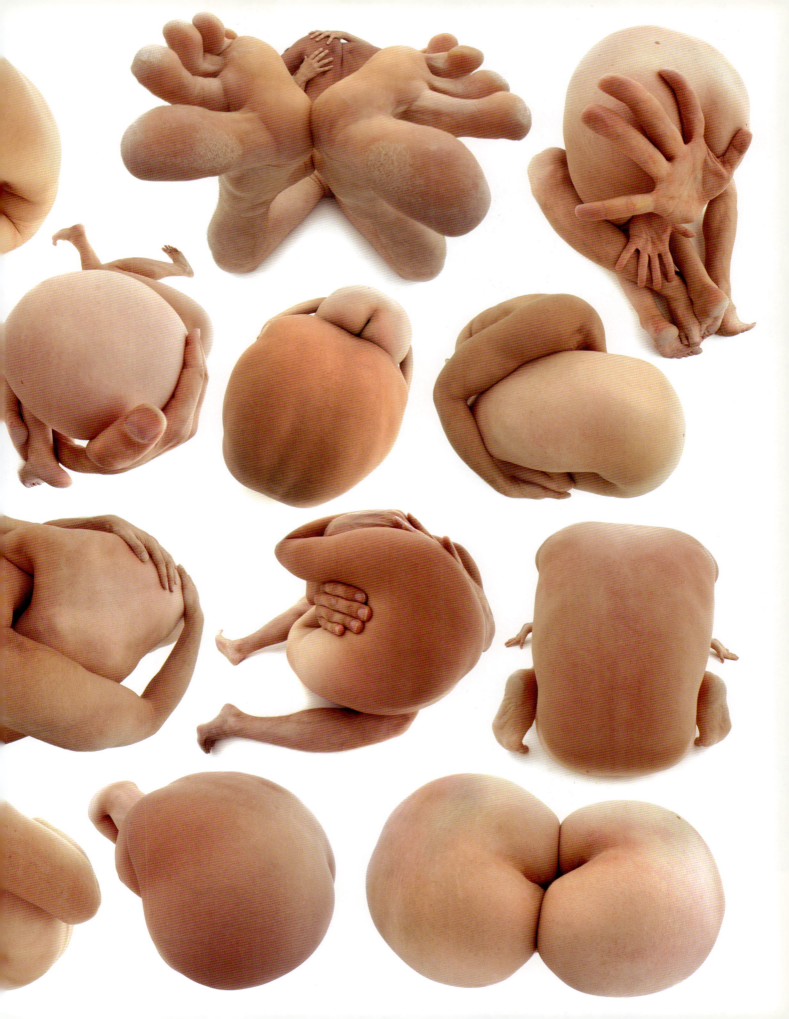

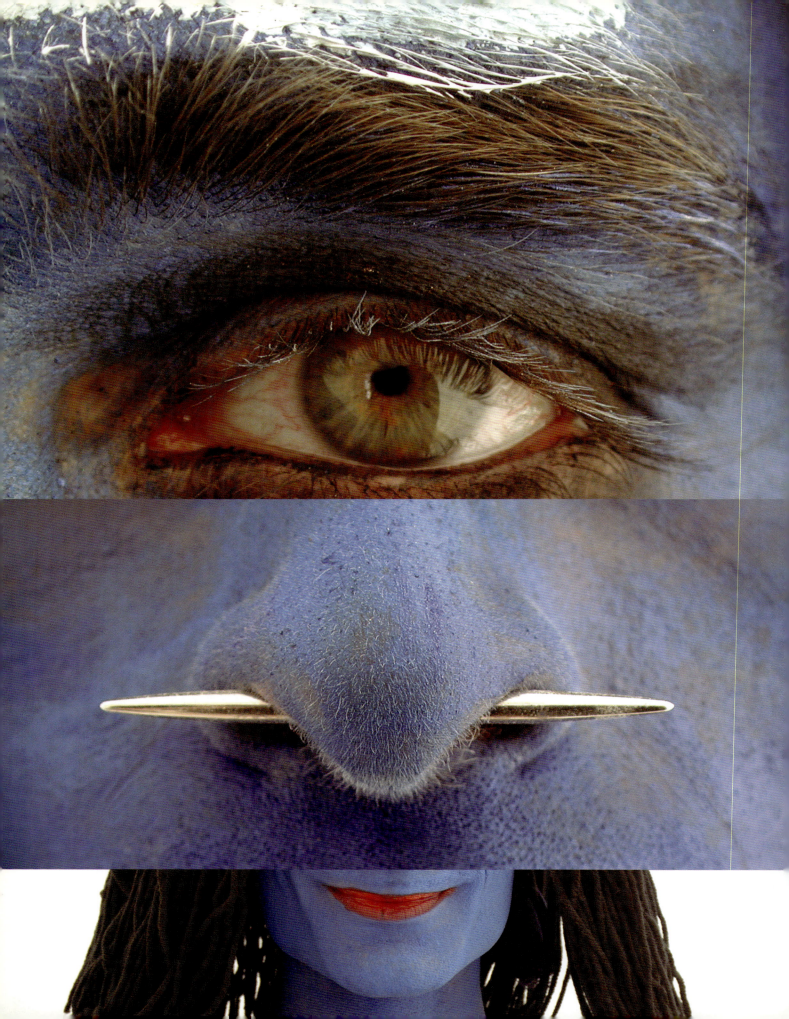

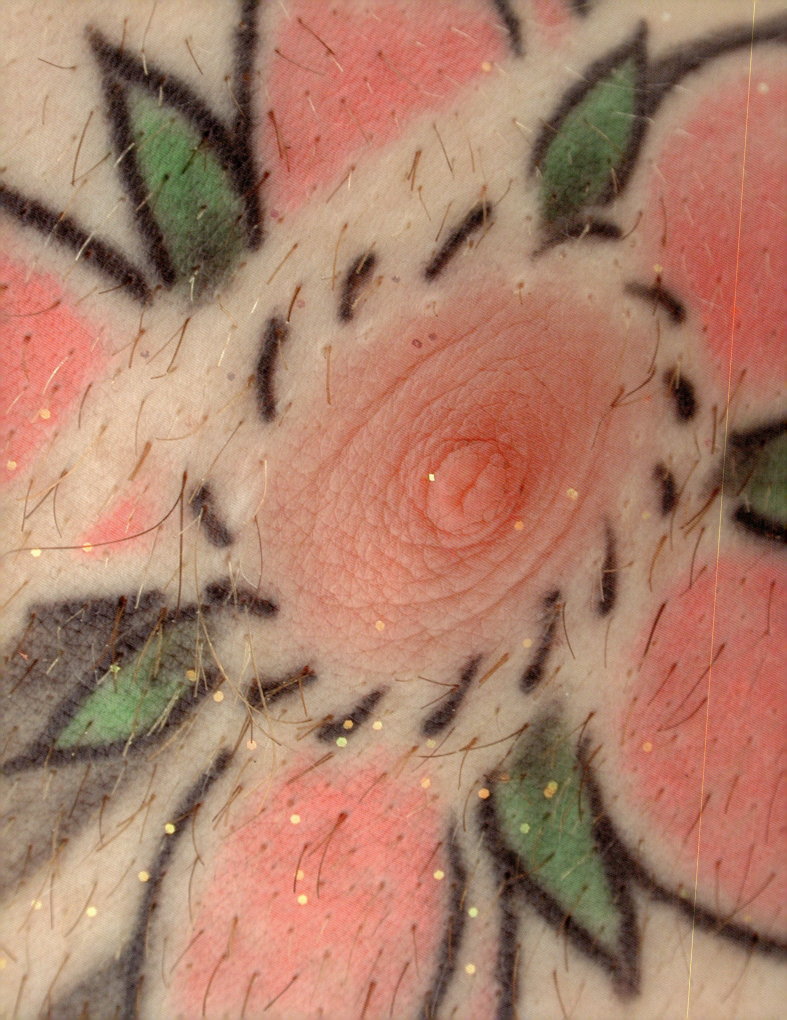

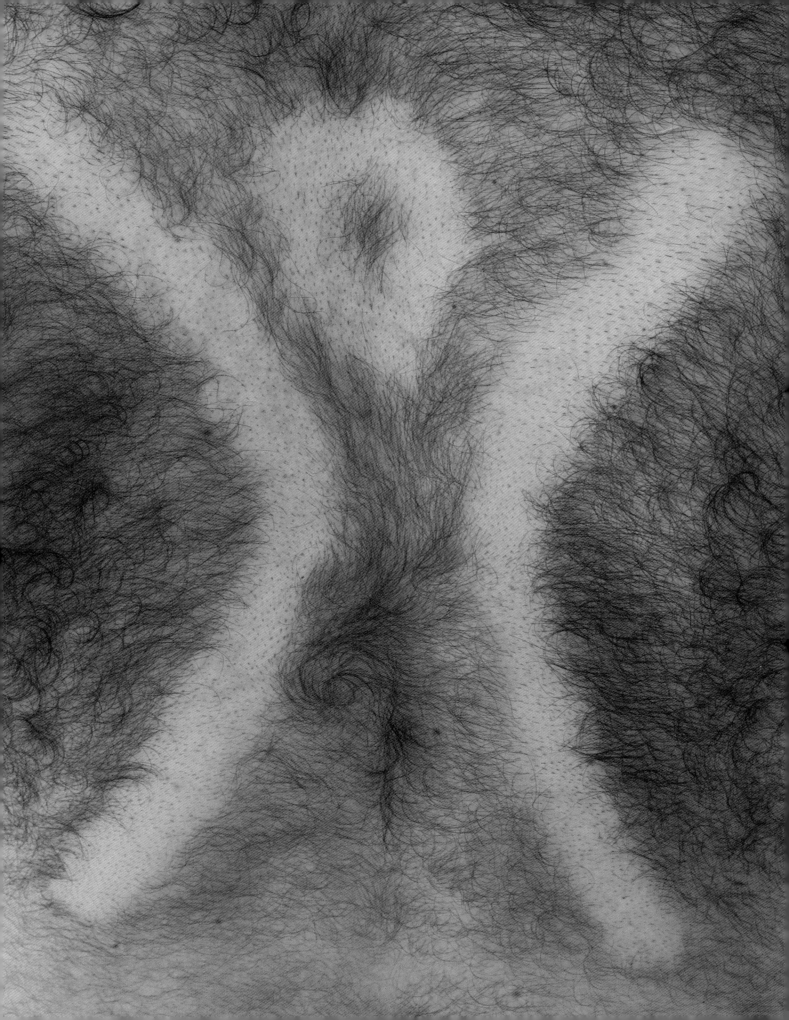

"I'm now in the process of restoring my foreskin."

"I heard that Prince Albert was uncircumcised and wore the ring through his penis head. I'm glad I have one."

"For medical reasons I was circumcised at age 23. I lost a lot of sensitivity."

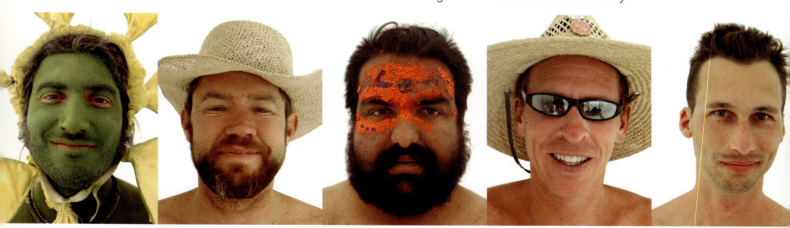

"After having two boys of my own, I finally thought about circumcision enough to be convinced I would not again."

"The uncircumcised penis remains more sensitive to touch and feeling. It is easier to achieve orgasm."

"I don't often think about it. It does seem unnecessary, but what custom isn't?"

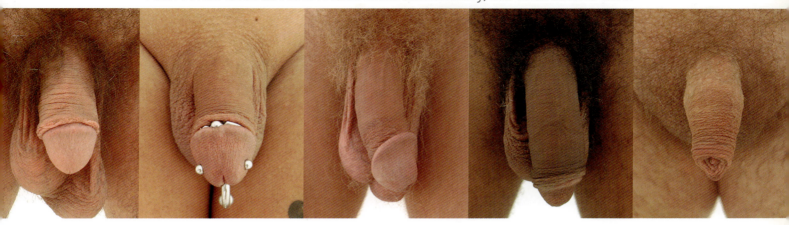

"I'm just glad I was too young to remember."

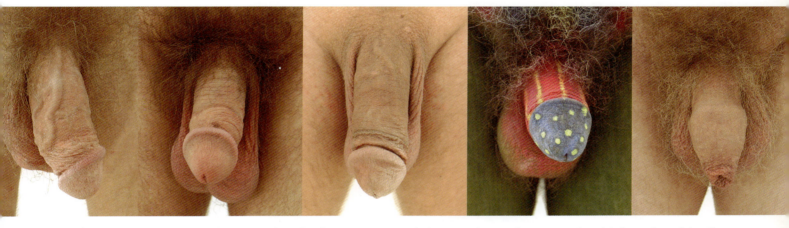

"Nobody ever asked me if I wanted it. Dad just continued the mutilation because they'd done it to him."

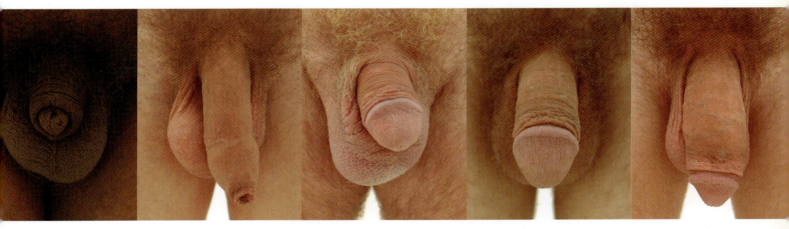

"I am truly thankful that the most sensitive part of my body comes with its own protective covering."

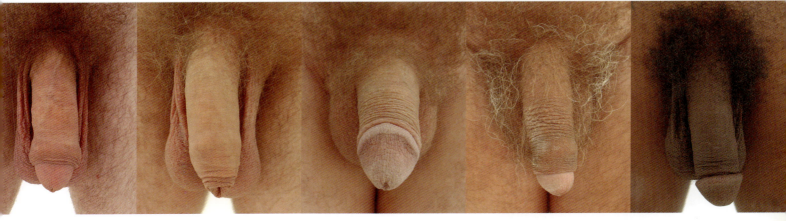

"I don't understand why this country has to automatically butcher little boys' genitals."

faces

Nurture your soul.
Your sensitivity.
Your strength.
Those who look in
your eyes will see it.

creation

There is no act more profound
than the act of creation.

A Gift From Todd

1. I, Julian, photographed sculptor and illustrator Todd Lovering in his silver city helmet. He made it out of foam. That's Todd to the right. He made that poster too.

2. Two years later, Todd emailed me and asked: would I like him to make a helmet for me? So I sent him back the sketches on the opposite page as a possible design.

3. At the next Burning Man, he presented me with this amazing work of art that lets me read minds and travel through time. That's me wearing it below. What a great gift!

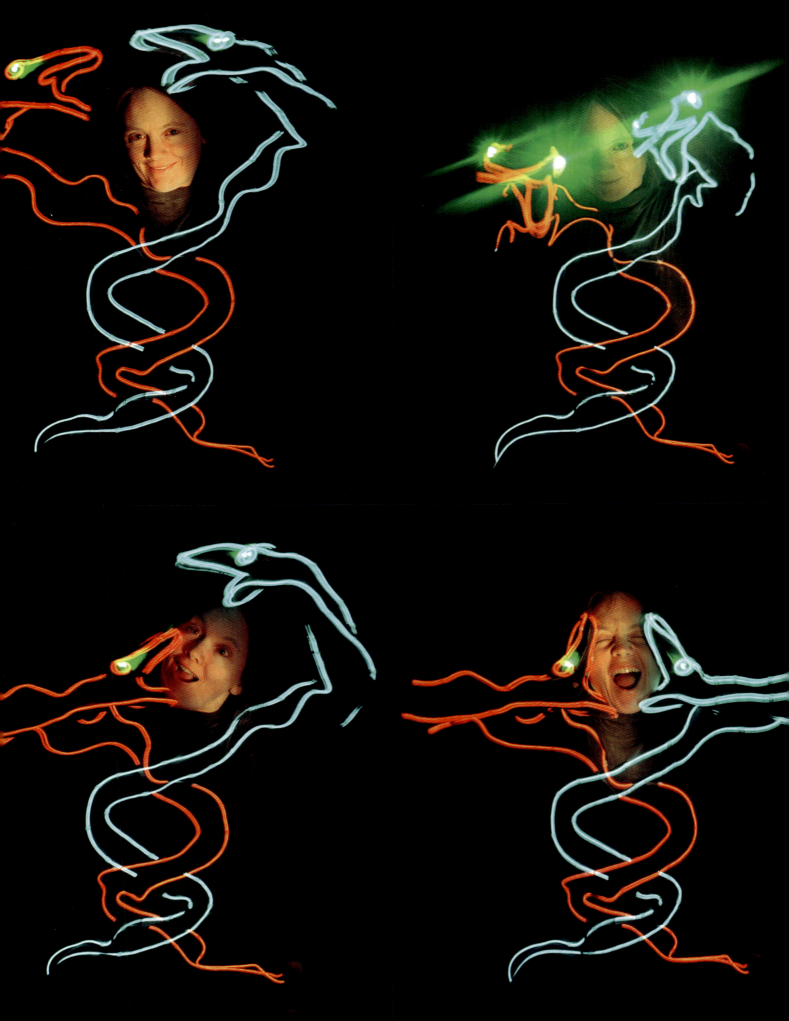

transformation

Who are you now?
Who are you going to be?

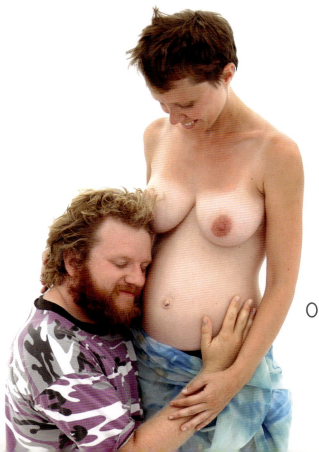

One year later...

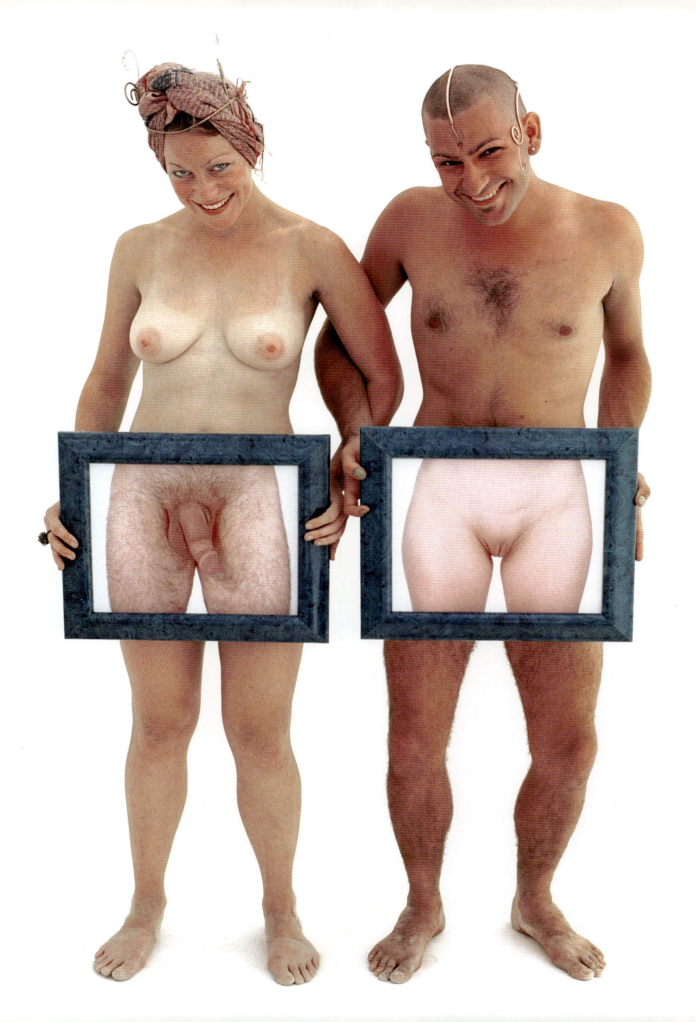

These are all the same person.

express yourself

Burning Man is an incredible canvas for self expression, but don't limit yourself. The place where you are right now is even more hungry for creativity, joy, and change.

the story of this book

This project was shown around to the big photo-book publishers by a seasoned agent. The publishers all said "no." They also asked to keep their copies! Despite their own interest, they said the content was too extreme, and that there would not be enough demand. It became clear that we were asking the establishment to publish something that was largely anti-establishment. So we appealed to the community, asking for enough funds to do the printing. Several hundred individuals pledged their support, so that within fifteen days we had already received the full amount. When the funding period was completed, the community had contributed well over the amount for which we had asked. This proved that there was a lot of demand and support for the project, and it enabled us to do a larger print run of a book of good length and quality. This print run exists thanks to the support of over 500 fantastically wonderful human beings, whose names are listed in these back pages.

Just as we went renegade in order to get printed, we are also planning to go for an alternative, yet powerful approach to spreading the word: It depends upon you to make sure that the world discovers this book.

What you hold is mere paper and ink, but if you keep showing it to new people, it will become a living thing, and the ideas will flourish, perhaps being reprinted into the future. If you find this project intriguing, show it to others, or get more than one copy so that you can give one away to a library or a friend. Point your friends to it online and see what they say. Thanks for taking the time to hang out with us on these pages. We hope to see you and trade hugs. Until then, you can visit us online at:

www.ThePeopleOfBurningMan.com

Julian and Jackie discover Burning Man

My name is Jackie Cash. My husband Julian took these photos, over the course of a decade. When we first came to Burning Man, there were fewer people around, and we didn't bring any gifts or art to share. Which is okay - it's hard to hit the ground running.

We happily immersed ourselves in all the art, performance, cutting-edge science, and general insanity. We were bowled over by all the talent and magic that had been dragged hundreds of miles and set up by volunteers, just for the participants to experience for one week. We understood quickly that it wasn't a show to watch: It was a game to join. In that sense, we had come unprepared, and it was very discomfiting to stand by and just be a tourist. We wanted to be a part of it, bring something, and share a talent or three. Julian immediately began dreaming up "theme camp" ideas. By the end of the week, Julian had formulated his plan. When we returned it would be as Supersnail, Portrait Photographer of the Playa.

One year later, we loaded our tiny hatchback with a studio and camping gear. We didn't have enough space inside the car, so we hung stuff on the outside. We strapped a long board to our rack and lashed eight huge plastic storage tubs to the board. We were as aerodynamic as a brick. Bystanders and drivers took pictures of our car, honked and waved as we drove from San Francisco to Nevada. We looked like a Supersnail for sure.

As it happens, that much wind resistance is a significant load. We were only partway along on our journey, when the support for the front rack snapped. At any moment, everything on the roof could have dumped into the Labor Day traffic. Luckily, we were able to pull off the highway and into a parking lot. Julian was in despair, the rack had been special order, and it was not going to be replaceable in time. He was losing a year's worth of planning, and all of his carefully saved vacation days. I kept it light and got us drinks as we turned over options. I recommend this approach to anyone: Keep it light, and keep hydrated. We were in the parking lot of a hardware store, so we decided to wander the aisles. There we found a packet of ratcheting tie-downs, guaranteed to hold several thousand pounds, more than the rating on our rack. We wound the straps through the windows and winched them tight to the ceiling. This tied the doors closed. We drove like that the rest of the way, 300 miles with the slipstream whistling in our ears, desert air flowing warm on our skin. We arrived at night, our headlights slicing the blackness, the road glowing a ghostly blue under the shimmering river of stars. The rich, sharp scent of desert sage rolled in the open windows – along with confused crickets and huge moths.

We arrived in the deepest hours of an August night. When the city came into view, I insisted it was another mining town because of its size and brightness. I held onto my amazed denial until we were rolling through Black Rock City proper. Waking in the chill of dawn, Julian got to work on building the photo tent. Leaving our camp would've meant losing a chance to photograph in the studio, so he sent me out to look for subjects. Wearing an ornate red Turkish costume with a striking fox mask, I scouted through town, approaching those whom I found interesting. I would stalk up to them and gently present my silent invitation, then bow, and hunt another. When I returned to camp, Julian was already photographing the folks I'd scouted, and there was a line out the door.

What happened next is what you see on these colorful pages. We connected with the artists, activists, do-gooders, do-badders, grizzled hobo sweethearts, and plenty of human beings with mundane jobs and vibrant souls. There was no Burning Man personality type, whatever historians might say in hindsight. The culture was unformed, whirling into being all around us. To be sure, there is more going on there, in one week, than can ever be seen or remarked. History is rarely so ephemeral as it is at Burning Man. Other photographers took care of landscapes and outdoor pageantry, science experiments and art pieces, dance and performance, fires and phenomena. Julian couldn't bear to let the people, their personalities and faces, go unrecorded. He fell in love with them. That's why they are so often smiling here – if someone falls in love with you, you can't help but be a bit pleased. But there is more to it, of course. What we found these people shared was a spirit of freedom and possibility. We all felt a strange ability to look each other in the eye and really *see*. We saw things we'd never seen before – maybe because we were looking. We tried as hard as we could to document that spirit, to show the ways it was making the souls of the people bloom and shine.

After that first year of shooting, many former portrait subjects asked to join our camp. They were great fun; we made many lifelong friends. Our book is very much a collaboration, in that Julian did portraits of subjects chosen by me and by the Supersnail campmates. They took over the tasks of running the camp and did them better. They developed a system for receiving the throngs who had been scouted – a path, signage, an area with a bit of shade. Visitors filled out consent forms inside the dusty green "greeter's tent," as bursts of random and hilarious mayhem emanated from a mysterious white cube next door. Some didn't know what they waited for, just that it sounded fun. We often had long lines. Julian was trying to give actual time to each person.

By necessity the studio tent was never shaded; it was often over 100 degrees inside. Julian wore full-length flannel pajamas, drank a lot of water, danced around in the searing heat, laughing with his new best friends. He brought out the best in people – and they brought out the best in him. He worked 12-hour days with, at most, 15-minute breaks. He was having such a wonderful time, he hardly noticed. In the daylight, surrounded by such remarkable folk, while making his art, he was an inexhaustible fount of joy. When the sun went down, the studio went dark, and Julian came out wincing as his body made its complaints known. By 7pm he would collapse in exhaustion, out for the night.

We spent nearly a decade with Supersnail Camp, and had many adventures. I had the most wonderful, joyous and deep experiences of my life in that city, and the same goes for Julian. Many things went wrong over the years. Black Rock City is a dangerous place. You can ruin your health if you don't take care of your body. Julian hit his knee with a sledgehammer. I was hospitalized for dehydration, and the same thing happened to Julian. My motto, suitable for framing in needlepoint, became: *"Never prove anything at noon in the desert."*

Our time at Burning Man was a learning experience. We learned our limitations. We learned caution. We learned to talk to strangers. We learned how to pack fast. We learned to be patient, even in the face of epic crankiness. We learned to give up grievances — even valid ones — and to accept each other as is. It was a great testing ground for our ideals and beliefs. We explored what worked for us, tried to hang on to what made us better human beings, and discarded what wasn't helpful.

So what is this book trying to express? Is it celebrating being contrary? Nekkid people? Irreverence? Well, sure, but that's concentrating on the most obvious aspects of a whole smorgasbord of ideas. Many of the most powerful pictures came from Julian contacting someone, saying "How do you want the world to be different?" and then working together on an image that could possibly transmit the idea and create that change. This is a collaboration with the revolutionary spirits of the People of Burning Man.

Why do we say they're revolutionary spirits? The people in these pictures are often caught in that moment when the soul shines out through the eyes. We wanted you to see this, their expressions, how they feel, their playfulness and their dignity. They aren't any one kind of person, but they're usually challenging something. They're often awake and evaluating the moment viscerally in a way I don't see often enough in my default world. The revolutionary quality we're describing is of the spirit, being awake in the present, choosing to be aware, expressive, and unafraid to see or be seen for who you are. Every generation has its own particular issues to tackle, but you can't fix what you can't see.

Revolution is distinct from rebellion. This book is not about being contrary for the sake of it, naked for the naughtiness, or irreverent to be rude. It's about challenging the things you need to challenge, following the rules you believe in, not just the ones you were told to follow. The American credo of "Sex, Drugs & Rock 'n' Roll" can be freeing, but that is simple hedonism. Real empowerment and freedom go much further. You don't need a partner, a band, or a substance to be free. While it is possible to do those things creatively, none of them *requires* creativity, and it is our belief that creativity and freedom go hand in hand.

Building the world you want to live in can start with a wisp of an idea. A little bit of your talent can be polished to a brilliant shine. All of these photos were shot by just one guy, hopping around inside the rickety little studio that you see on the front page. Sharing our talents has made all the difference. It made us more ourselves. We don't pretend to speak for all Burners, but we hope that this collection of images embodies what Julian and I found valuable out there: Making stuff, self expression, questioning authority, spirituality, innocence, joy, being good to each other, pushing boundaries, and a not-quite-safe giant hamster wheel that shoots 20-foot flames.

Burning Man is an incredible canvas for self expression, but don't limit yourself. The place where you are right now is even more hungry for creativity, joy, and change. This book wants to be your counter-culture spirit guide. We hope you'll use it to inspire your own adventure. Blow your own mind! Express yourself — there is a light in you, and if you let it shine, your inner brilliance will help others find their way. Be brave. Be free.

julian & Jackie Cash

To see websites that go with these and other stories, hop to: www.ThePeopleOfBurningMan.com/stories

 Julian Says: "I made this sign. I love illustration as much as I love photography."

 As a Burning Man Founder, visionary city planner, and dedicated community leader, Larry Harvey loves thinking up neat ideas, nurturing them, and then seeing them come to life.

  His wife of eight years had just left him. He had been letting his hair grow since they'd married.

 $teven Ra$pa is behind this mirror which reflects myself, and Harrod Blank with his movie crew. Their film documents the various artists and their art projects, including me and my project, held by **you**.

$teven Ra$pa

    The bloody doves were $teven's response to the wars. Note how his beard grew quite long during the years we created photographs together at Burning Man.

 This is Water Boy. Left: Marque and Maria. They are dangling in a custom created water filled rubber suit. You can see Julian and a crowd of onlookers in the reflection at the bottom.
Right: Marque as Bucket Head.

 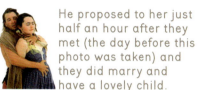 He proposed to her just half an hour after they met (the day before this photo was taken) and they did marry and have a lovely child.

 This project intensified the next year. Masks were given to participants to wear. Synchronized music and instructions were heard inside the giant heads. Following these instructions together, the masked ones seemed to dance as a coordinated and mystical troupe.

 Marcy and Griffin gifted me the light toy and I outlined them. To see more "light paintings" see EdibleLight.com

 Three armed ladybug jacket created and worn by Matt and Rachel.

 This image was used for the cover of the Italian version of "Yoga for People Who Can't Be Bothered to Do It" by Geoff Dyer. The colorful performer's name is Helvetica Bold.

 The Billion Bunny Oath: "I freely and hoppingly renounce my dirty stinking messed up carcass of failed and foibled humanity, in order to evolve as a sentient furry being. I hereby come over to the bunny side. I will HOP. I will wiggle my tail. I will deliver colorful eggs to the masses and support a universal campaign of fluffy goodness and jellybeans for all. HOORAY!!!"

 Most vehicles don't actually fit into the studio, so I'd improvise other white environments. For this shot I hung white tarps off the side of a box truck and laid other tarps on the ground. For other shots, an awesome camp (Black Rock Refinery) provided 25' tall white walls.

 The other animals are real. This one is fake. :)

 This man does "Ferret Rescue" in Empire NV, a town not far from the Black Rock Desert where Burning Man is held.

 Our Supersnail campmate Julia "Cthulhia" Tenney is playing and didn't suffer. She makes psyanky eggs and coffee-based watercolors. She's been working on a series of "infinite halo" Tarot Cards for 14 years.

 "Would you like a clean hug or a dirty hug?" With his giant pink Swedish Massage cuffs, Halcyon offers to pound your back. Upon request, a hidden crotch vibrator could add to the excitement. A camp mate of mine said she had her first public orgasm this way.

 "These are both the same man. He was doing a social experiment: One day he was covered with truly negative symbols, but behaved very kindly and courteously towards everyone else. On another day he was decorated with friendly symbols, and he was hostile and rude. Acting as the "nasty" guy he came close to being escorted out of Burning Man. In both cases, people reacted more to how he behaved than to his symbols.

 Those are actually his own credit cards. Special effects make-up by Randal.

www.ThePeopleOfBurningMan.com/stories

Yes, they cashed the check. Photo taken before the whistle blew on the WorldCom scandal. He had dozens of checks with him that were each their own unique art projects. After seeing his checks on the web, I had sent him an odd postcard. The return address listed only my website. He showed up at Burning Man two years later with his checks, and the post card I'd sent him.

The woman on the top is vegan. The woman on the bottom is vegetarian. Her boyfriend isn't.

Julian says: "I love the flag and all that I believe it stands for. To me it represents the freedoms that are our rights in the US of A. I believe that the flag directly symbolizes the freedom to do extreme things, such as burning a flag. It is not more important than the freedoms it represents."

These were his personal possessions. He lugged them hundreds of miles out to Burning Man for this photo. The televisions are plugged in and working. His chains were tight enough to draw blood.

I hollowed out a TV and put a mirror in place of the screen.

The multi-talented Randal painted this globe for us. It is uncommon to find a globe with no political boundaries shown.

A woman wrote me about modeling this image. On the appointed day, the model arrived already painted blue. I thanked her, sent her to get stars painted on, and we created this fantastic photo! Chatting with her later, I found out she was not the woman that I'd arranged the shoot with. The original contacted me later to apologize for being a no-show.

Doom Squad Apocalyptic Cheerleaders
Camp Nip Nip Nip
Commissary
Documentation Crew
Dragon Crew
Sky People
"Random" people
Camp Nip Nip Nip
Porn Clown Posse
Fluorescent
PAN
Cafe Espresso Tech Crew
Nuclear Family
Senior Staff (mostly)
Cafe Staff
Maids
Black Rock Spatial Delivery
Lust Monkeys
Lamplighers
Supersnail This camp created this book.
Cayote Pack
Rangers

Sky diving photos by Thom Van Os

Key women who make/made the Burning Man event exist, and function. From front to back: Maid Marian, Crimson Rose, Actiongrl, Harley K. Dubois, Dana Harrison, Holly Kreuter

Ministry of Statistics
Stats are from 2003

Pranking is an essential part of Burning Man culture. After their shoot, they flounced over to the Center Camp Cafe. They pretended to be snobby clueless fashion models, who'd been flown in for a product shoot. It was a great prank. People fell for it and mayhem ensued.

The Petermans are incredible! They helped make Hushville, created the renowned Playa Chicken, and are always creating interesting new projects to prank or inspire us all.

Sculpture by Laurence Cook. Snakes on Pillars painting by Wesley Anne. Over the week of the event, the artists and passerby filled the sculpture with different types of money. As the sculpture was consumed by flame, the burning money flew all over.

Photo of the Burning Man Burning Up by Ashley Niblock,

Ryon Gesink and his giant flame throwing wheel dubbed "Th' Fuck Machine".

Jeremy Faludi

Ggreg Taylor

The Women of Thunderdome

DrMegaVolt: "In 1996, some members of Survival Research Laboratory built a cage to protect a person from Tesla coil currents. I got inside the cage as a stunt. Surprisingly, I felt no sensation of electricity while inside. The current flowed outside of a conductor, isolating the interior from dangerous electric fields. Eight months later I decided to shrink the cage down around myself and create a metal suit that allows mobility." Don't try this at home.

www.ThePeopleOfBurningMan.com/stories

 These hardy DPW (Department of Public Works) folks showed up for our scheduled shoot despite the intensity of the dust storm. That's a DPW dog. Other dogs should never be brought to Burning Man. It's not a dog-friendly environment.

 Before this shot I was nervous about the jump. He assured me he'd done it thousands of times and it was quite safe. After the accident he said the white interior of the studio threw him off his spatial bearings. I was profoundly upset that he got hurt. I do my photography to help the world.

 After this photo was taken, Jackie got so badly dehydrated, that she still has heatlh problems when the heat is over 90°F (32°C). From this incident came the mottos: "Keep it light and keep hydrated" and "Never prove anything at noon in the desert."

 Fakir Musafar gave himself his first piercing at 12 years old. Here, just days before his 70th birthday, he demonstrates a Sun Dance style of bodily sacrifice. His research and exploration into body modification and shamanism birthed much of the Modern Primitive movement.

The desert is harsh. Do not bring babies or go to Burning Man while you are pregnant unless you know what you're doing, have gone before, and have talked with other women who have done it. There are significant risks. , Be careful. Be aware.  Rachel was pregnant this first year that I met her and Jeremy.  These shots were taken with their healthy baby one year later.

These are pictures of the glorious participants of the Critical Tits bike ride. They were photographed in many different groups, and the outstretched hands of the people on the end of each group was made to touch. If this image were to be printed life size, it would run the length of a city block.

 These are members of Sporosite camp. They help to adorn willing bodies by spraying them with liquid dyes. The dye is safe commercial food coloring.

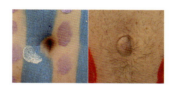 Going through the book, can you find who these two belly buttons belong to? The second one is near the end of the book.

These are all the same people.

  Formal outfits were protected from dust by sealed plastic bags until the time of the photo session.

 Shots of Yogi Scott and Delta taken with a 12mm fisheye lens. If you like these, you will enjoy the photography book "Body Knots" by Howard Schatz.

Randal as Shiva.

 Tongue dyed green.  Aaron's nipple. Back fur.

 Quotes are all thoughts from those men about circumcision. Images of the men are in random order.

 This photo was taken by Randal. There is something so timeless about bare asses in chaps.

 Nicole Johnson helped run The Berkeley Free Clinic, where work is done to prevent the spread of HIV.

 This photo was on the cover of Rolling Stone Italy in June 2004. Sandy's costume of disembodied hands was created by Peter Hudson in a multi-step casting process. Peter has also made a series of 3D zoetrope sculptures that must be seen to be believed.

 "Venus of Willendorf". Figurines of this goddess date back to 22,000-24,000 BC.

 Leighton Kelly performed with The Yard Dogs Road show. He's a clothing designer at Five & Diamond.

www.ThePeopleOfBurningMan.com/stories

 Food dye was used as body paint. Some dye got under his contact lenses.

 Peeka Pete has his initials on his front teeth.

 The brightness of the studio often makes for small pupils.

 These are both Christina Preston.

My wife

Jackie is my love. She's cuter than the furriest of wombats and smarter than the Seven Scintillating Scholars. An incredible editor of words and pictures, she has lived this project with me.

Also Jackie

An Indian friend saw this and said "That looks like one of my gods."

Mannequin.

The Mannequin Head says: "Jackie likes stickers and patches".

Science is creative

You are profoundly incredible, Todd!!!!!

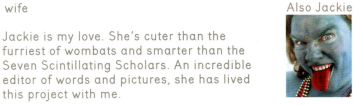

For 24 hours, he was completely blind. He often had to depend on the kindness of strangers.

Electroluminescent Wire

Snake puppets by Bridget Hardy.

 A telestereoscope increases the distance between your eyes. This enhances your depth perception. It makes reality seem even more three-dimensional..

 These two amazing authors are not shown elsewhere in the book, but are worth a mention. "This Is Burning Man", is a fascinating chronicle of Burning Man and its characters, by Brian Doherty. "Burning Man" is a beautiful collection of photos by the talented Vincent Huang.

Since the city is about 2 miles across, it's useful to have a bike.

 They are holding framed photos.

The same man

These are all Fleeky Flux
F is for Fleeky, Flexible & Fun!

Randal is an omnipresent genius of costumery and theatrical make-up. He is a fabulous photographer and model. He has helped me and this project greatly with food, design, and, of course, his wise counsel.

 This is Nifer burning an old photograph of herself. The match was held in the split of her forked tongue.

The Sephiroth, Tree of life.

I love collaborating with publications that help spread the message in yummy ways!

This book was created thanks to the direct support of these incredible, fantastic and monumentally awesome people:

Hibbard Engler
Sheeri Cabral
Noirin [nəˈdʃɪk] Plunkett
Tellman
Yasmine S. Mehmet

Donna Eck
Andy Chan
Matthew Wickline
Miss Joule
Alan Macias

ChickenJohn
Michael Brodesky
ZPS
Robn Parsons
Martha Phoebe
Andie Grace
Anne Easley
Will Chase
Roxane Williams
Halcyon
Grandpa Caleb
Nifer Fahrion
Aaron Muszalski
Karie Henderson
Dan Shick
Nicole Johnson
allegra lundy
Ira Goldman
Destin Gerek
Don & Michelle Marker
(allie "sandwich" barden)
Kim Corbin
Natalia Mozdzen
Ouchy The Clown
iKandi The Clown
Doctor MegaVolt
Mistress MegaVolt
Affinity Mingle
MonkeyBoy
Barbara Sicuranza
Chris Stein
Mark Solomon
Christopher Schardt
Paul David
Kerry Miller
Simone Paddock
Tracy Bugni
Dale Ghent
Sheera Duerigen (matt, laura, ellie, and doug)
Schwern
DearGodNo
Phil
Mayhem
hntr
Jing Jing
Tony Cabral
Bobby Wheelock

Debra Tramontini
Hayley Serafin
Julian Assange
daMongolian
Annie Sprinkle
Joe Polish
Mike Cline
Danny Frank
Eben Pagan
Wyatt Woodsmall
Joe Polish
Mike Cline
Wyatt Woodsmall
Helle Rytkonen
Markus Andersson
Karen Blicker
Brenda Lee
Deanna Tiberg
David Fink
Kim Clark
Harvie Branscomb
Benjy Feen
Denise Cottin
Matthew A. Schultz
Angela Dawn Schultz
Casey West
Anna Salyers
Dana Harrison
Torti Geri
(Texas Joe of BDC&WB)
Doc Pyro & CJ
Ed Mechem
Lonn Johnston
Megumi Bell
Bleys
Simone&Katie
Richard Dice
Robin Kells
Rudy Moore
Molli MacDonald
David LaMacchia
Jennifer Waggoner
(Mikey "AgentEye" York)
Sara Sullivan
Victoria Sebanz
Andrius Smitas
MaRika
(Brian Halpern "Nipper")

Lois Flynn
Eff Norwood
Abi kelly
DnA from the AEZ
flint
kristie
Matisse Enzer
jet
drue
Marcy Swenson
Dale Larson
(Joan "Battle Kitten, Kitty" Mentanski)
Jane "Trouble" Nemis
Jungle Jim
Jungle Bus
Suzan with a Z
Volunteer Tom
Tiger
Kitten
Rob McNicholas
Rebecca Weinstein
Snakie Lady (Bridget)
Noca
Voodoo Space Patrol
Pope Rajulio
Katie Napalm
little dragon
Kate Monster
MARTIN DUNCAN
COLINE MALIVEL
Toni Sartorelli
(Angelique Nash-Thurmeier)
Ranger Wee Heavy
Ranger Foofurr
Safety G
Scamper
Jim Taflinger
Durwood Pepper
Victoria Kearney
James Woodbury
Eric & Rebecca
Andrew & Mona
John R Taylor
Natalie Isford
(David William Grimsby)
(Morgan Nicole Grimsby)
MidKnight

(Koko Ra Mokee Molaki)
Ashley Niblock
Susan Jennings
(Glen M. W. Trowbridge)
Billy V Vaughn
Peter the Hun
Jeff Woods
Tim Brown
Lizzie Robles
Kip
Cat Herder
(Joshua "H3R3TIC" Martelli)
Killian Hamlin
Mike Perez
Amanda McCormick
Maxime
Mike Kidd
Mike Nova
Bashie Waggoner
Marcy Blue Wachter
Mystic Cat
Kabotron
(Tiahaar Kurtheru h Sarock)
(Kisho Crubo S K D Saaj)
(Mark and Shiree Schade)
Lee Chubb
Sarah Chubb
Alain Bloch
Tabitha Donaghue
Duke of Weimar
Eno (Pedro)
Scott Meyer
(Andy Teuteberg, aka Teuty)
(Crashy Pants Jackson)
Sachi Ivy
(Janss & Susan Franden)
(Monkey Pirate Pirate Monkey)
Heidi Gallues
(Anthony "Noodle" Gallues)
The Ginsburg Family

The Cobb Family
(RouseMouse Of Contraptionists)
Violet Blue
Kerrie & Jörg
Ranger Beavis
Reverend G
Cpt. Smashy & Dr. Jet
Fred cutler
(Alison MacRae-Miller)
Berm McCandless
Terry "Sunny" Tholl
Pink Flamingo Camp
Joel
Sheva & Nicky
(Tanya "freak" Thompson)
(Ken "Hot Plumber" Flournoy)
sweet doodlie doo
Babs
Keith Grote
John & Susan
Arturo
Michael Coulter
Mark Waites
(Ranger Bassomatic Xcess)
Ranger Freefall
(Nichole *Lady* Rovello)
(Jessica *Kanga* Button)
Kara Kytle
(*~firefly~*)
Annette Kytle
Nelz
stephanie
Laura La Gassa
Shirley Myers
Hazel Motes
Leslie Ayres
(Stephanie Renee Peebles "PEEBS")
Yogi Scott
Stewart Smith
Mark
Cyn Lee
Lisa Boulanger
Jen Jobart

(Matthew Noble Marker)
Patrick
Susan Larcombe
sara raintree
(Matt "HazM@" Morgan)
Mad Hatter
(John "Jocko" Magadini)
Retro
Grant Gouldon
Mel, Bill, Chey & Nick Sundberg
technopatra
Annette M MacLean
Amylisa Parker
Nelehuj
Dan Girellini
James Saunders
Zucky
Maria Rangel
AMP & RKane
Bob Bobo
Rangepunk
Tamara Munzner
Miss Delta
Kimberly
Zach
Noodlebarbarian
Bruce Bieberly
ABQ
(Brian "thepartycow" Walsh)
Eli Larin
Madelynn Martiniere
wygit, aka Michael Cox
Rig Dady
Keith Carroll
BigFoot
Davee Evans
Carla Everett
Murray Schane
Jen Upchurch :)
hudzo
Ballistic
Gadget
Dennis Bartels
(Chris DogFish Wippern)

David Lindes
Gina Ferrante
BoyScout
mr.blue
Marvin Gardens
Twan
Sister Mable Syrup
J Johnson
Eric Baron
(Rufus Xavier Sasparilla)
Louise and Phil
Major Tom & Kite
StewedArt
Richard Law
Julia Brown
monsi & mups
Shane
Barbara
Kurt D. Yardley
beth grundvig
Hjalmar Kristiansen
Amelia Gilley
Ari Schindler
Steven R. Triano
Tim Schapker
Sabrina Lo & Paul "Cowboy" Wanveer
Megs
Rob Lord
ted redelmeier
Jim Schrempp
Dr. Mercury
Roger Giles
PONCHO & PONCHO
Mikey
David Orias
Jess Hobbs
Ken and Linda
Eric O'Neill Parks
Other White Meat
Fawn
Kelly
Enyala
Paul Fenwick
Wade Scribner
(Steve "Ronin Sherpa" Williams)
Marsha Grant
Roberta Dayal
Mick and Max Icke
VaVa Vunderbust
Jody Wasend
Elizabeth Letcher
krahnik blis
Georgie Rebane
Justin Eastman
Joshua Marker
Barnaby Fry
Epiphany Jordan
Jeff Zelnio
Cory Mervis
Kimberly Daugherty
Kate Gille
Janet K Miller
Jason Sylvester
William Magdziarz
Jessica Miller
Holly Kreuter

Alysia Crissman
Douglas Wolk
John Windberg
thomas heavey
Carol Gunby
Ted Altenberg
Matthew Litwin
Harold Baize
Shaun Botha
Marcy Protteau
elyssa marsland
David Solito
Mark Maxwell
Orlando Wood
Josh Hildebrandt
Sarah Sevilla
R. L. Mirto
Andrew Hammond
Shawn Brower
Tony Peacock
Michael Baas
(Cara Dorenzo Carvalho)
Dale East
Sarah Burcham
Johnney Josefchuk
Suzanne Jarvis
Ivan Cash
Michael Barrett
Sylvia
Lehte Rickard
Julie Cash
Craig Cooper
paolo pedrinazzi
Rob Wynne
(David Law c/o Thomas Prunier)
Mikey Siegel
Elinoar
John Brennan
Thibeaux Lincecum
Mark Gibian
Kristi Hart
Chris Kantarjiev
Jeff Lindsay
Robert Zverina
Helen O'Neill
Stephanie Gutzman
Scott Beale
Roy Feague
jason rusoff
Kevin Beals
Sven Myren
Grant Patterson
Aaron Price
Stephanie Fairbanks
Andy Tibbetts
Daniel Price
Linda Weiss
Scott Shaw
Fred Owsley
Marc Harris
Wendy Goodfriend
Angela Taylor
Rod Coleman
Mary Waterfield
Lee Wherry Brainerd
David Eisenmann
Christine Ring

Libby Murphy
C. Maness
james squires
Mike Osborne
Charles Lemmon
Jan Sysmans
Carla Diana
Dominique Hatt
David Martin
Ray Trent
Kirk Hargreaves
Howard Davis
tony lee
Luke Ryan
Stephan Moore
David Ogawa
Mark Young
Manuel Díez
Gregory Fung
Brock Yancey
Mike Prasad
Brody Scotland
Yani Wood
Tonia Wierzel
Rei Yoshioka
Erika Czerwinski
Cary Riall
Edward Ingraham
Alon Sagee
Paula Jo Povilaitis
Christopher Olewnik
James Kuhn
Aaron Mandel
Joev Dubach
Ronnie Brust
Michael Fasman
Susan Logsdon
(Tally Fruchtman Rossiter)
Jessica Schafer
Allison Cruz
Thea Izzi
silvia stephenson
Marni Nemer
John Archdeacon
Lauren Klein
Vincent Kitirattagarn
BLAZE FLOYD
Naomi Hamby
David Mandel
Kristina Fiorini
Richard Gooding
Laura Prisbe
(Laurel Sparks Burkhalter)
Vic
Janet Voss
Susie Kameny
Brian
Wendi Joiner
Michael J. Lowe
Christopher King
sylvan cornblatt
Jeff
Julie Holabird
Katrina Glerum
(Laura L. Ansley-Cavaliere)
Ron & Cher Mandel

Diamond
Ron DePugh
Meredith Mull
Bruce D Greenspon
Barbara Fried
Daen de Leon
(Robin Shepley-Shornstein)
Dan Shornstein
Michele Berg
Hank
Matt Ho
Josh Rafofsky
Lukasz Waszczuk
Chris Quaintance
Chris Weitz
Alex Jahnke
Jared Hirsch
Michael Perez
Adina Rose
Patrick Auld
Trampas Thompson
Jeanne Fleming
duane peterson
Daniel Gluesenkamp
Jay Kearney
Elsye Walker
scott alan
Jason Dorfman
David Rogers
Joe Bamberg
Don Butler
Stephen Fawcett
Lorene Flaming
Roy Isserlis
Matt Sponer
dr deb windham
Obie Fernandez
Ryan Johnson
Colleen Campbell
Inga Small
Susan Goldberg
Garret Alfert
Kevin & Leslie Merritt
Robert W. Dickerman
Richard Aplin
Dan Becker
Allan R. Dick
Shawn Ferry
Alex Botkin
Ian Knutila
Erik Bos
(mecca and george manz)
beth & john threlfall
Quinn Dombrowski
Fred Abou Jawad
JOHN ST CYR
Tristan Horn
Carrie Kattermann
Eddie Ojeda
Steve Hecker
Liz Molitor
Kyle Grow
Bill Barclay
Stuart Berger
Bob VanDerSluis
ALEX N. GANSA
Viola Toniolo

Deborah Wallach
Natalie O'Halloran
Wendy Marussich
Simon Amar
Erin Johnson
Molly Ditmore
Justin Powers
Josh Kleiner
Hans Roos
Ryan Koga
HOPE Art
(Samuel M. Coniglio, IV)
(Tanya Brum Da Silveira)
megan tennity
Sarah Johnson
Eric Arvidson
Eric Herrmann
Lori Duvall
John Kelly
Tamara Davis
Victor Vorski
Jane Greenbaum
Lisa
Nion McEvoy
(Giedrius Kavaliauskas)
Jairo Marin
Jimmy Frith-Brown
Molly Denevan
Tree
Kristine Enea
Paul walker
Brandon Eversole
Tommye Maddox
Hadley Taylor
Todd Weinstein
Scott Cocking
Craig Latta
Jewellee Dalrymple
Peggy Ozol
Anya Kozorez
Walter Reuschle
alexander filatov
Brian Wendt
Patricia Glenn
Charles Gadeken
Angela Fernandez
Stanley Sagov
Cindy Fawcett
(Mike and Colleen Dillon)
Shiny Disco Ballz
Krazy
Jay Kravitz
Margaret Lambert
Robin H. Johnson
Margot Stewart Esq.
Yasmeen E. Stewart
Joe Gardella
rocketgirl
Dave Jennings
Sachi Denison
John Tupper
Suzie Sims-Fletcher
Bert
Jett Atwood
Lisa D. Eller

Sam Young
Ron Halbert
Jerri Manthey
Danger Ranger
Harley
Niffer
Amacker
Tiara Saurus
Danese Cooper
David Marr
Neon Bunny
Janet Mayeaux
John Mosbaugh
Jennifer Waggoner
Glynda Cotton
James Kuhn
Kerry Miller
Karen Malka
Matt Ho
Dale Tegman
Professor Violet
Jungle Jim Gibson
Nicole Maron
Quinn del Baile
Keith Phillips
Marcy Protteau
Simon Clark
Aldo Mosca
Scott Beale
Stephen R. Scaffidi
Wade Scribner
Plumeria
Angi Cecilia Doyle
Robert Easley
Christine Kristen
Kate Stillings
Bill Hunter
Libby Murphy
(M.A. Baas "Brotherluv")
Eric Baron
Josietayloris
Sydney Cash
Grace Ubiera Marty
Dr. Anne Churchland
kirk mickelson
Tracy Bugni
Tomy Huynh
Natalee "Zote"
Ted Beatie
The Professor
Jenifer Hope
Sarah & Geoff
Stephanie Andrews
David Vernon
Christine Moore
Bryan Sebastian K
Eddie Codel
Peter Leung
Wagner
Courtney King
Amanda McCown
Stephen Paulson
Fabi Elias-Ramsey
Janice Ross
Scott Hunt
Dominic Tinio
Randal Alan Smith
Simone Paddock

To see websites that go with these fantastic people, hop to: www.ThePeopleOfBurningMan.com/credits

Burning Man
For more info see: www.BurningMan.com

The Collaboration Requests
Many photos came from collaborations that started with: "How do you want the world to be different? What image will help make the world change in that way? Together we'll make that image."

Using the Images in this Book (Republication)
These images being used and shown in many places can be a super goodness. For info on getting permission, see: ThePeopleOfBurningMan.com/reuse
To discuss possible republication, chat with Julian
julian@JulianCash.com

Credits
For more information on this book, see www.ThePeopleOfBurningMan.com

Photography (and lots else in this book) by Julian Cash www.JulianCash.com All photographs copyright Julian Cash 2011 (except where noted).

Listed are photo credits and any creations made specifically for the book project. Most of the editing and design was done by Julian Cash, Robert Easley, Jackie Stewart Cash, Veronica Van Gogh, Eso, Randal, Megan Cash, Splat/Dave Le, Jeff Lester, Laura Martin, Dan Shick, Ted Altenberg, Allegra Lundy, and Kelsey Ahern. Randal did the credit card head makeup, painted world globe, TV eyeball, and Sephiroth body paint. Jackie drew the fetus on the pregnant woman, the tug-of-war breasts, drew the picture of us driving to Burning Man, and kept me going endlessly. Burning Man on Fire by Ashley Niblock. Temple burn photo by Jason Chin/Julian. Photo of Julian with the Todd Lovering helmet by Sebastian Banker. Bert Adams did airbrush work for "Meat is Murder" and other painted people. "Pledge" excerpts from article by Stephan Clark of Record-Bee. Stats by Ministry of Statistics. Anyone who created art represented in this book keeps all rights to that art. Any logos, brands etc., remain the property of their respective copyright, trademark, etc. holders.

Massive thanks to...
All the people I collaborated with in the studio, Jackie Jack, Randal, Patrick Gavin, Sam Young, ChickenJohn, PK, Molly + Aaron, Jeff Lester, Robert Easley, Kelsey Ahern, Katy Bell, Ggreg, Veronica Van Gogh, Susan + Ashley, Starboy, sandwichgirl, Hammer Pants, Courtney + Roy, Rebecca, Jessica Palopoli, Cory, Davel, Cliff, Sebbo, Charlotte, Julia, Dan Shick + Nicole Johnson, Joshua Marker, Kash + Melissa, Anna + Jeff, Ted Beatie, brYan, The Yard Dogs Road Show, Morgan, M.I. Blue, Robin, Michelle Savage, Megan, Meghan, my sister Megan Cash, mother Sharron Loree, father Sydney Cash, brothers Ivan Cash + Elliot Cash, Andy Chan, Tamara, Julie Brodeur, Gluesenkamp, Carrberry, Dori, Llyra, Rachel, Halcyon, Donna Eck, Simone Paddock, Robn Parsons, Natalia Mozdzen (ZPS), Liz + Chris, Kim Skipper Corbin, Sheeri Kritzer Cabral, Wendy Boswell, Wendy Goodfriend, Noah McPike, Jungle Jim Gibson, Kerry Miller, Jim Miller, Sara, Lori, Kwai, Misty, Aimee', Eva Destruction, Dattner, Dale Larson, Praveen, Mark Solomon, Todd Weinberg, Edward Oleksak, Margot Stewart, Steven Raspa, Harley, Marcia Crosby, Holly Kreuter, Maid Marian, Larry Harvey, Nurse, LadyBee, CameraGirl, Frog, Bex, Action Girl and all the others who helped bring this project to fruition.

Legal Notice
The appearance of the following logos, brands, nations, publications, etc. are not intended to imply an endorsement or connection between themselves and this book. *Free to Be You and Me, Dirt Devil, Dust-Off, The Real Mother Goose, The Bible, Star Trek, Planned Parenthood, San Jose Metro, Rolling Stone, 7 Dance Club Magazine, Wells Fargo, Target, Bank of America, Chevron, MasterCard, Yahoo, Visa, MCI WorldCom, Fight Club, Warner Brothers, Isreal, Palestine, Jamaica, The Confederacy, The USA, The US Federal Reserve, The Boys Scouts of America.*

Photography Info
I don't like to use digital effects on photos to make them different from what I experienced, though I did link the outstretched hands of The Women of Critical Tits. Photographs were taken in a tent against a white paper backdrop with all natural light. The pictures span 1998 to 2004. 35mm film cameras and digital cameras were used.

Don't lose your shirt
People working on big projects for Burning Man have a tendency to spend far more money than they plan to, or ever should. Be wi$e! In fact, the 60K I spent on this project became the topic of an IRS audit.

The good stuff
Love, respect, creativity, bravery, and joy.
Do what you can to improve the world.
A dozen dozen hugs,
Yet more love, julian

ISBN: 978-0-615-46954-6
Library of Congress Control Number: 2011926212
Images © Julian Cash 2011 (unless stated otherwise)
Printed in Hong Kong By Regent Publishing Services
Union Artist Press (UnionArtist.com)